בִּרְכוֹת שֶׁל שַׁבָּת

Shabbat is a time of peace, a time for family. There are special בְּרָכוֹת with which we welcome Shabbat into our homes. When we say בְּרָכוֹת over the candles, wine, and hallah, we are thanking God for creating the Shabbat and allowing us to celebrate it.

Practice reading the בְּרָכוֹת aloud.

1. בָּרוּךְ אַתָּה, יְיָ אֱלֹהֵינוּ, מֶלֶךְ הָעוֹלָם, אֲשֶׁר קִדְּשָׁנוּ בְּמִצְוֹתָיו וְצִוָּנוּ לְהַדְלִיק נֵר שֶׁל שַׁבָּת.

Praised are You, Adonai our God, Ruler of the world, who makes us holy with commandments and commands us to light the Sabbath light (candles).

2. בָּרוּךְ אַתָּה, יְיָ אֱלֹהֵינוּ, מֶלֶךְ הָעוֹלָם, בּוֹרֵא פְּרִי הַגָּפֶן.

Praised are You, Adonai our God, Ruler of the world, who creates the fruit of the vine.

3. בָּרוּךְ אַתָּה, יְיָ אֱלֹהֵינוּ, מֶלֶךְ הָעוֹלָם, הַמּוֹצִיא לֶחֶם מִן הָאָרֶץ.

Praised are You, Adonai our God, Ruler of the world, who brings forth bread from the earth.

NAME THE SHABBAT OBJECT

Complete each sentence by writing the English word or drawing a picture.

Blessing #1 is said over the	Blessing #2 is said over the	Blessing #3 is said over the

לְהַדְלִיק

to light

נֵר

a light, candle

שֶׁל

of

שַׁבָּת

Shabbat

LIGHTING THE CANDLES

The first Shabbat בְּרָכָה we say is over the candles. Saying the בְּרָכָה helps us usher in Shabbat with brightness and joy. Once the candles have been lit at sunset and the בְּרָכָה has been said, Shabbat has begun.

Practice reading the בְּרָכָה.

בָּרוּךְ אַתָּה, יְיָ אֱלֹהֵינוּ, מֶלֶךְ הָעוֹלָם, אֲשֶׁר קִדְּשָׁנוּ בְּמִצְוֹתָיו וְצִוָּנוּ לְהַדְלִיק נֵר שֶׁל שַׁבָּת.

Praised are You, Adonai our God, Ruler of the world, who makes us holy with commandments and commands us to light the Sabbath light (candles).

MATCH GAME

Connect the Hebrew word to its English meaning.

to light	בָּרוּךְ
light, candle	שַׁבָּת
Shabbat	נֵר
praised	לְהַדְלִיק

UNSCRAMBLE THE PRAYER

Write the ending of the candle blessing in the correct order.

בָּרוּךְ אַתָּה, יְיָ אֱלֹהֵינוּ, מֶלֶךְ הָעוֹלָם, אֲשֶׁר קִדְּשָׁנוּ
בְּמִצְוֹתָיו וְצִוָּנוּ . . .

_____

DID YOU KNOW?

Do you know why we light *two* candles on Shabbat?

The Ten Commandments appear twice in the Torah.

The first time—in the Book of Exodus—Adonai tells us: *"Remember* the Shabbat."

The second time—in the Book of Deuteronomy—Adonai tells us: *"Observe* the Shabbat."

The two candles remind us of both these commandments.

Some people light more than two candles. In some homes candles are lit for every member of the family. There is no limit to the number of candles you can light.

CANDLES AND LIGHT

Candles and light play an important role in Judaism. The Ḥanukkah candles flicker and glow on your window ledge. We light a *yahrzeit* candle to remember the anniversary of a loved one's death. And the Eternal Light always burns above the Holy Ark.

Practice reading each of these blessings recited over candles.

1. בָּרוּךְ אַתָּה, יְיָ אֱלֹהֵינוּ, מֶלֶךְ הָעוֹלָם, אֲשֶׁר קִדְּשָׁנוּ בְּמִצְוֹתָיו וְצִוָּנוּ לְהַדְלִיק נֵר שֶׁל שַׁבָּת.

2. בָּרוּךְ אַתָּה, יְיָ אֱלֹהֵינוּ, מֶלֶךְ הָעוֹלָם, אֲשֶׁר קִדְּשָׁנוּ בְּמִצְוֹתָיו וְצִוָּנוּ לְהַדְלִיק נֵר שֶׁל יוֹם טוֹב.

3. בָּרוּךְ אַתָּה, יְיָ אֱלֹהֵינוּ, מֶלֶךְ הָעוֹלָם, אֲשֶׁר קִדְּשָׁנוּ בְּמִצְוֹתָיו וְצִוָּנוּ לְהַדְלִיק נֵר שֶׁל שַׁבָּת וְשֶׁל יוֹם טוֹב.

4. בָּרוּךְ אַתָּה, יְיָ אֱלֹהֵינוּ, מֶלֶךְ הָעוֹלָם, אֲשֶׁר קִדְּשָׁנוּ בְּמִצְוֹתָיו וְצִוָּנוּ לְהַדְלִיק נֵר שֶׁל חֲנֻכָּה.

5. בָּרוּךְ אַתָּה, יְיָ אֱלֹהֵינוּ, מֶלֶךְ הָעוֹלָם, בּוֹרֵא מְאוֹרֵי הָאֵשׁ.

Do you recognize the blessing over the Ḥanukkah candles?

Write its number here. _____

FOOD FOR THOUGHT

A blessing is usually said *before* the action takes place. For example, when we eat an apple, first we say the בְּרָכָה (...בּוֹרֵא פְּרִי הָעֵץ), and then we take the first bite.

But in the case of the Shabbat candles, we light the candles *first* and say the blessing *afterward*.

Why?

Once we say the blessing, Shabbat begins. Many people will not light a match on Shabbat. Therefore, first we light the match (and the candles), and then we say the blessing.

PRAYER DICTIONARY

בּוֹרֵא

who creates

פְּרִי

(the) fruit (of)

הַגֶּפֶן

the vine

BLESSING FOR THE WINE

The Kiddush is the בְּרָכָה we say over wine. קִדּוּשׁ—Kiddush—comes from the word that means "making holy." This בְּרָכָה helps us sanctify Shabbat and make it holy. Traditionally, before the Shabbat קִדּוּשׁ is recited, we fill the wineglass to overflowing to thank God for our abundance of blessings. In the Shabbat קִדּוּשׁ we express our joy as we remember two occasions—when God created the universe and when we were freed from slavery in Egypt.

Complete the following activities for the blessing over the wine.

בָּרוּךְ אַתָּה, יְיָ אֱלֹהֵינוּ, מֶלֶךְ הָעוֹלָם,
בּוֹרֵא פְּרִי הַגָּפֶן.

Praised are You, Adonai our God, Ruler of the world, who creates the fruit of the vine.

1. Circle the word that means "fruit."

2. Draw a box around the Hebrew word that means "who creates."

3. Underline the word for "praised."

4. Write the English meaning of מֶלֶךְ. _____

5. Put a star over the word for "the vine."

6. Write the part of הָעוֹלָם that means "the." _____

7. Write the part of הַגָּפֶן that means "the." _____

8. What is another English word for "the fruit of the vine"?

_____

6

BLESSING FOR THE BREAD

On Shabbat, we also say הַמּוֹצִיא—the בְּרָכָה for bread—over the specially braided ḥallah to praise and thank God for giving us food to eat. Remember that there are בְּרָכוֹת we can say before eating any kind of food—breakfast cereal, a cheese sandwich, or even your family's special chicken dish!

Practice reading הַמּוֹצִיא.

1. בָּרוּךְ אַתָּה, יְיָ אֱלֹהֵינוּ, מֶלֶךְ הָעוֹלָם,
2. הַמּוֹצִיא לֶחֶם מִן הָאָרֶץ.

Praised are You, Adonai our God, Ruler of the world,
who brings forth bread from the earth.

DID YOU KNOW?

Bread is the symbol of food in Jewish life.

In the Bible there are many examples of guests being offered bread to eat. Abraham and Sarah, who are famous for their hospitality, immediately served bread to make their guests feel welcome.

In fact, bread is so important that one blessing said at the beginning of a meal—הַמּוֹצִיא—covers all the food to be eaten during that meal.

PRAYER DICTIONARY

הַמּוֹצִיא

who brings forth

לֶחֶם

bread

מִן

from

הָאָרֶץ

the earth

WORD MATCH

Match the English word to its Hebrew meaning.

A. who brings forth   מִן ( )

B. the earth   הָאָרֶץ ( )

C. bread   לֶחֶם ( )

D. from   הַמּוֹצִיא ( )

UNSCRAMBLE THE PRAYER

Write the ending of the בְּרָכָה in the correct order.

בָּרוּךְ אַתָּה, יְיָ אֱלֹהֵינוּ, מֶלֶךְ הָעוֹלָם . . .

מִן   הַמּוֹצִיא   הָאָרֶץ   לֶחֶם

_____

An Ethical Echo

In the Book of Deuteronomy there is a passage that says "Befriend strangers, for you were strangers in the Land of Egypt." What better way is there to welcome strangers than to open your home to them? The mitzvah of *Hospitality* (הַכְנָסַת אוֹרְחִים—*Hachnasat Orḥim*) is made greater when you offer your guests food and drink.

Think About This!

A new student joins your class in the middle of the school year. What can you do to befriend this stranger?

THE HOLIDAY CONNECTION

As we begin to tell the Passover story at our seder, we uncover a plate of matzah and lift it up for all at the table to see. As we recall that our ancestors ate this "bread of affliction" when they were slaves in Egypt, we announce: "Let all who are hungry come and eat."

Think About This!

Why is the mitzvah of *Feeding the Hungry* (מַאֲכִיל רְעֵבִים—*Ma'achil Re'evim*) so closely linked to our lives in Egypt? How can we fulfill this mitzvah?

הַבְדָּלָה

Do you remember how we welcome Shabbat into our homes? We say בְּרָכוֹת over candles, wine, and ḥallah. There's also a special way that we say goodbye to Shabbat—with the Havdalah blessings.

הַבְדָּלָה means "separation." When we say the Havdalah blessings over wine, sweet spices, and a special braided candle, we are separating the uniqueness of Shabbat from the rest of the week. These blessings thank God for allowing us to celebrate Shabbat and ask God to help us remember its holiness throughout the next six days.

Imagine how you feel on your birthday. It's a special day, when everyone gives you extra attention with gifts, good wishes, and cake. Even when it's over, you can keep that wonderful feeling with you all year long by looking at photos or watching a video of your birthday party. It's the same with הַבְדָּלָה—the scent of the sweet spices and the bright light of the candle help us keep the Shabbat feeling with us all week long.

Practice reading the blessings over the wine, the spices, and the lit candle.

בָּרוּךְ אַתָּה, יְיָ אֱלֹהֵינוּ, מֶלֶךְ הָעוֹלָם, בּוֹרֵא פְּרִי הַגָּפֶן.

Praised are You, Adonai our God, Ruler of the world, who creates the fruit of the vine.

בָּרוּךְ אַתָּה, יְיָ אֱלֹהֵינוּ, מֶלֶךְ הָעוֹלָם, בּוֹרֵא מִינֵי בְשָׂמִים.

Praised are You, Adonai our God, Ruler of the world, who creates the varieties of spice.

בָּרוּךְ אַתָּה, יְיָ אֱלֹהֵינוּ, מֶלֶךְ הָעוֹלָם, בּוֹרֵא מְאוֹרֵי הָאֵשׁ.

Praised are You, Adonai our God, Ruler of the world, who creates the fiery lights.

Now read the blessing that separates the holy day of Shabbat from the other days of the week.

בָּרוּךְ אַתָּה, יְיָ אֱלֹהֵינוּ, מֶלֶךְ הָעוֹלָם, הַמַּבְדִּיל בֵּין קֹדֶשׁ לְחוֹל, בֵּין אוֹר לְחשֶׁךְ, בֵּין יִשְׂרָאֵל לָעַמִּים, בֵּין יוֹם הַשְּׁבִיעִי לְשֵׁשֶׁת יְמֵי הַמַּעֲשֶׂה. בָּרוּךְ אַתָּה יְיָ, הַמַּבְדִּיל בֵּין קֹדֶשׁ לְחוֹל.

Praised are You, Adonai our God, Ruler of the world, who separates the holy from the everyday, light from darkness, Israel from the other nations, the seventh day from the six days of work. Praised are You, Adonai, who separates the holy from the everyday.

Think About This!

Why do you think we need to separate Shabbat from the other days of the week?

FLUENT READING

Practice reading the lines below.

1. וְשַׁבַּת קָדְשׁוֹ בְּאַהֲבָה וּבְרָצוֹן הִנְחִילָנוּ.

2. וְשָׁמְרוּ בְנֵי יִשְׂרָאֵל אֶת הַשַּׁבָּת,
לַעֲשׂוֹת אֶת הַשַּׁבָּת לְדֹרֹתָם.

3. בָּרוּךְ אַתָּה, יְיָ אֱלֹהֵינוּ, מֶלֶךְ הָעוֹלָם,
עֹשֶׂה מַעֲשֵׂה בְרֵאשִׁית.

4. בְּרֵאשִׁית בָּרָא אֱלֹהִים אֵת הַשָּׁמַיִם וְאֵת הָאָרֶץ.

5. אֲדוֹן הַשָּׁלוֹם, מְקַדֵּשׁ הַשַּׁבָּת וּמְבָרֵךְ שְׁבִיעִי.

6. בָּרוּךְ אַתָּה יְיָ, מֶלֶךְ עַל כָּל הָאָרֶץ.

7. מְקַדֵּשׁ יִשְׂרָאֵל וְיוֹם הַזִּכָּרוֹן.

8. זִכָּרוֹן לְמַעֲשֵׂה בְרֵאשִׁית.

9. טוֹבִים מְאוֹרוֹת שֶׁבָּרָא אֱלֹהֵינוּ.

10. בָּרוּךְ אַתָּה, יְיָ אֱלֹהֵינוּ, מֶלֶךְ הָעוֹלָם,
אֲשֶׁר קִדְּשָׁנוּ בְּמִצְוֹתָיו וְצִוָּנוּ לְהַדְלִיק נֵר שֶׁל שַׁבָּת.

Artist: Ilene Winn-Lederer; Photographs: Creative Image (5, 11). ISBN 0-87441-751-1 (Brachot shel Shabbat); Manufactured in the United States of America.
ISBN 978-0-87441-1751-7